THE EASE ERA

THE EASE ERA

The Juvenile Oligarchy
and
The Educational Trust

by

PAUL MALLON

WM. B. EERDMANS PUBLISHING CO.
GRAND RAPIDS 1945 MICHIGAN

THE EASE ERA *by* PAUL MALLON

PRINTED IN THE UNITED STATES OF AMERICA

THE EASE ERA

The successful devastating exposure articles of Paul Mallon which broke the rule of progressive education

and brought

the promotion of sound value in handling juvenile delinquency and education in every city of this land.

Preface

"FOR there shall be a time when they will not endure sound doctrine, but according to their own desires they will heap to themselves teachers, having itching ears, and will indeed turn away their hearing from the truth, but will be turned unto fables"—Paul (2) to Timothy.

That time was certainly December 31, 1943. I had listened to the speeches and the published advice of the prophets of false modernism to their teachers with itching ears, and their fallacies of thought which even a six-months old baby could (and many did) penetrate to their own advantage, until I could not longer restrain myself and composed an article which I believed set forth sound, modern psychiatric doctrine in connection with juvenile delinquency. I wrote it as a holiday column at a time when news was slack, and in it I questioned the primary basis of psychological advice then being spread to the exclusion of all others, by Mrs. Roosevelt, Mayor LaGuardia, Senator Pepper, the spinsters of their Children's Bureau, and others of that ruling oligarchy of well-meaning loose theorists, holding philosophically that the way to handle juvenile delinquency was to "let them eat cake" literally. I felt positive they did not know what they were talking about, but were following a general political fad of the day to raise the ideal of ease in effortless learning and loose child management. "Let baby do as she wants" and "sonny, not mama, knows best" were their lines. At the same time they directed their corrective efforts against juvenile delinquency to the spending of more money for playgrounds, whereas it seemed to me delinquency was already apparent in the vast playgrounds we had. They had a sound political remedy for themselves in the spending of money but not a remedy for delinquency. It was their youth-doctrine I thought was wrong. The playgrounds needed intelligent modern psychological leadership, not more swings.

I was prepared to have my viewpoint completely engulfed by an avalanche of protesting letters to my editors, for there had been no expressions in any way similar to mine in general circulation at that time. I was astonished at what happened. A crescendo of approval rose up from incoming letters on my desk. It came from teachers eager to give me evidence of the truth of my assertions, professors of psychology in such eminent institutions as Temple University, a member of the National Board of Examination for Psychiatrists, a Reform School Superintendent in Pennsylvania, the

Mayor of Atlanta, the police in a New Jersey town, a member of the School Board in San Francisco, and so on — not fan mail, not crank epistles, but urgent incontrovertible evidence upon which to build my thesis in detail. For two years it continued to pour in. I weighed it as it came, checked the other side of it, ascertained the valid facts, presented them, and became, to my complete astonishment and without my desire, an unpremeditated crusader for the institution of sound values in youth management and education.

My newspapers, many Parent Teachers Associations, Boards of Education, and finally some religious leaders of various persuasions, took up these points and pressed them home for reforms in their own localities. President Sproul of California University, March 23, 1944, assailed the "Progressive Craze", and announced tightening of the elective system at his school of higher learning. Teachers underscored certain sentences of articles pertinent to their local school conditions and thumb-tacked these slyly on the school bulletin boards. The high school professors in Atlanta signed a Declaration of Independence from Progressivism, as inspiring a document as you have ever read (you will find it in these following pages).

A corrective national movement was started. It is still on, still expanding, although it has far yet to go.

My method at the outset was not one of direct assault, but more that of sifting and analyzing the false doctrines, so as to appeal to any objective-minded man with proof that this rabbit education (as Dr. Nicholas Murray Butler called it) could NOT be right. Later I was subjected to some persecution (none of it effective), but irritating and somewhat costly. Several of my best newspapers were induced to quit my column, or print it infrequently, or move it to a more obscure position but most of them defended and expanded my stand with great results in their localities, and really accomplished the results. I was subject to attack behind my back in localities beyond my reach. You will learn the details of one or two instances in subsequent pages. So some of my observations got a little less objective toward the last.

The few papers which quit have not come back. This collection of my columns solicited by at least 500 persons in unsolicited letters to me, was refused publication by every large New York publisher when submitted by my syndicate, King Features. My name bears anathema yet in some extremely progressive quarters, where diabolical things were suspected of me, and the story of the wholly innocent beginning, and thoroughly fair and American continuance of my crusade will not be believed. Some doubting editors still click their teeth dolefully at my departure in this case from my usual duty of News-behind-the-News reporting.

Yet I have felt no emotion but clean glee that my snowball grew as it did, and I would not change or erase a speck of it.

This I sincerely believe: The thought-origin of progressive education, its inspiration, pervaded every field of human activity in the ease era. We similarly got away from sound values, not only in child raising and education, but in international politics, where the given-word in treaty form was made to be broken, where faith in Christian ethics no longer existed. We got away from it in our own domestic politics to a considerable extent, and in business. Contracts were made to be broken. Honor was not respected. Success justified any loose course. We also veered away from sound values in finance. We destroyed the morality of money and promoted every financial artifice to escape sound facts in every direction.

That era is drawing to a close. Men cannot live that way. There is a yearning in them which requires them to believe sincerely in God, and accept Christian ethics. You cannot substitute worship of the state or admiration for sly finesse. These false gods will not inspire men to do the job of life well, or bring the desired results to men economically, financially, politically, or any other way.

Christianity lays down a system of ethics essentially sound, not only in a spiritual way, but as a way of material life for men in dealing with each other. What good are treaties if not based on faith and honor, and where are faith and honor guaranteed firmly outside of Christian ethics? Pagan ethics cannot establish faith. Economically Christ taught work was good — "By the sweat of thy brow." Work makes production. Production is the dynamo of economies. Therefore, Christian economies are essentially sound. Genuineness was also a basic principle of Christ. He discarded all that was false, synthetic, unnatural. He taught soundness.

This is the only solution for the world. There is no other road to travel. We do not need to "get back to

Christian principles," as some say. We need to go forward with them. We must accept them and apply them to our enlightened modern knowledge. There is no real basic conflict between science and Christian ethics. No invention of medicine challenges the spiritual anatomy of the human soul. Science and religion are truly interdependents. Hypochondriacs can actually be cured by faith and work. The only question is whether we must tread the path of degradation, which we have been following, until chaos exposes its absurdity to every thinking man in complete collapse of all values, or whether the shock of war may have furnished the opportunity for men, that they needed, the mental shock which will restore an appreciation for sound values all along the line.

I am no preacher. I am a reporter. As such I see signs that the turn may have come, that the era of unsoundness, the ease era, the progressive paganism of those with itching ears, may already have passed for the great bulk of the people, who, themselves are already going forward with Christian principles in their own lives.

PAUL MALLON

Washington, June 1945

Contents

ADULT ADOLESCENCE

1

ADULT ADOLESCENCE

THE incontestable answer to all this juvenile delinquency in the news is one word — Discipline.

This is not old-fogeyism, but ultra modern psychiatric doctrine. The instinctive tendencies of children must be curbed by discipline until they have reached the age where self-restraint enables them to conform to social customs and to take advantage of social opportunities.

Too many parents and children themselves erroneously believe that modernism permits free expression of their instincts. This leads to the current savage eyesores of our vaunted civilization in which prostitution has been flaunted conspicuously in cities by grade school girls, thefts and crime before the age of reason has been reached, and murder of parents by children who find them troublesome.

The fault is *not* with modern principles, but that they are not enforced. Toleration of such popular misconceptions is the crime of our age. I have seen in Times Square, New York, girls barely past puberty with soldiers and sailors, not in small groups, but in droves, while police look on shaking their heads in apparent helplessness. I could break that up in 15 minutes. Everywhere that soldiers and sailors go, there are MPs. If the military police were ordered to detain and question every serviceman accompanying a girl of doubtful age, and terms in the guardhouse were provided, the practice would soon lose its current trend.

The experts on this subject of juvenile delinquency, even including Mrs. Roosevelt, all think in social grooves apparently, proposing only that more and more money be spent for boys clubs, playgrounds, social workers, psychiatrists in police courts, etc. After they get all those things done, they will still need the answer — discipline.

The home is still the cradle of our culture. Discipline should be re-established there on modern psychiatric lines. If the home is broken up by parental delinquency (which also is widespread) or by the war, or for whatever cause, discipline will have to be exerted somewhere else. We could start by restoring it to the schools. Nowadays, teachers are afraid to touch the poor little dears. I know one school teacher in whose four junior high school classes, only 50 percent are up in their work today, the remaining half being delinquent. She cannot make them work. Her hands are tied by modern misconceptions of science against just punishment in any effective form.

If the restoration of home and school discipline is not enough, the churches are the next power that might be able to use some.

By all means, use of such power, and in fact all youth leadership, must be kept away from the State, particularly the federal government. Now is the best time in the world to judge what state discipline will do, with fresh evidence of what Hitler and Mussolini did in brutalizing their little Nazis and Fascists. We will have none of that here. Nor can you get discipline by expansion of social work or ex post facto punishment in juvenile courts. The place to start is in the beginning, and someone will have to do it, parents, schools, churches, perhaps all three.

THE BEST MOTHERS

2

THE BEST MOTHERS

THE Pepper sub-committee held loud hearings on juvenile delinquency some weeks back. Mayor LaGuardia fulminated. Nothing came of it. If anything does, you may be sure it will be an idea for spending money. That is the politicians' answer to every problem.

The mail reaction to some thoughts I ventured (December 31) suggests the solution might be wrought without the expenditure of a Morgenthau penny simply by some public leadership along the right path. This leadership could well be undertaken by LaGuardia, Senator Pepper, Mrs. Roosevelt, and other major politicos already articulately involved.

The personal testimony in letters from school teachers, soldiers, mothers, fathers, would make a large sized volume, but it all boils down to a simple understanding of what has taken hold of us nationally. It shows the symptoms of the trouble, points to the cause and the cure.

Teachers wrote many specific case histories of their inability to handle the problem of an increasing number, but still a minority, of children. The large majority still comes from sound homes where good mothers enforce discipline. These are probably being better raised today than any children in our history. They do their work and conform to the customs of society.

But there are literally hundreds of thousands, if not millions of homes in which there is a degrading and degenerating absence of discipline — not due to economic reasons either, as the prim social thinkers and politicians contend, but solely because the woman of the house, or the man (generally both) is indifferent to the responsibilities of child raising and stupidly, lazily, self-interestedly maintains no discipline over the young. They are the ones who are spawning the new class of hoodlums. While this class may number considerably less than 10 percent of the mothers today, they have weakened the moral strength of a whole nation and their brats will soon be begetting other brats to be similarly raised wild under the paternal excuse of self-expression.

The problem is to reach that class with intelligent, modern conception of responsibility, or otherwise enforce discipline upon that non-conforming class through the schools and the churches (but not the state). The currently popular way in Washington is to coddle these miscreant matrons with excuses that their husbands may not be making enough money, and similar rot. The best mothers I have seen have been in the poorest homes, and the best men I have met have come out of those poorer homes.

To make them measure up, the first necessary step is to have the current leaders change their tune. Customs and popular thinking are very largely established by personal leadership of prominent people (including writers) who set an example and suggest the general norm. If they would stop sobbing sympathies, and preach family discipline, the pressure from the top would be reversed. If they strengthened this with a warning that undisciplined children will be disciplined in the schools, enlisting the leadership of Parent Teachers Associations (the mothers on those boards are never the parental delinquents) and strengthen the hands of pastors in the churches as well as the teachers, to do the job that parental delinquents will not or cannot do, then these children running loose would soon find it to their advantage to conform to an enlightened civilization of average American youth.

I will have more on this subject later.

INTELLIGENT PUNISHMENT

3

INTELLIGENT PUNISHMENT

THE person who is as much to blame as the delinquent parent for juvenile delinquency is the widespread fool — male or female — who thinks disciplining of the young is reactionary victorianism or old fogeyism. This is the one who furnishes the necessary excuse for both the delinquent mother and child, and corrupts our satisfactory average.

No psychiatrist or philosopher in all history has ever said an adolescent should be allowed to express himself freely without discipline. Where these foolish people get mixed up is that they do not understand the difference between discipline and punishment. The best discipline may never need punishment. If discipline were perfect, there would be no reason for punishment.

Nor does punishment mean that every little Joe Doakes should be taken out to the woodshed every hour on the hour — or perhaps at all. Punishment must be intelligent. That is all modern mental science teaches, as I get it. It is truly old-fogeyism, it is worse, it is a crime — for irate parents or teachers to flail youths unjustly, unfairly, indiscriminately.

Punishment can be more effective in a thousand other ways than with a switch or ruler. It depends on the child. The denial of something a child dearly wants could be a worse blow to him than a strap across his or her pants. Punishment should differ as widely as personalities differ. It must only to be effective — that is, corrective.

Modern psychological science merely teaches that the Victorian methods of physical punishment were more often unintelligent than not, indeed sometimes expressed the sadism and mental deficiency of the donor. Overlordly and exasperated parents could ruin a child's mental outlook for life with unintelligent punishment. That was a crime against society. It had to be changed. But it is a far greater crime today to rush to the opposite extreme and seek to abolish both discipline and punishment. It is greater because it creates such situations as we are involved in today.

Inhibitions is another misunderstood word. Popular tomfoolery holds it to be a calamity for anyone, even an adult, to have an inhibition. Is a parentally induced inhibition against adolescent girls having sexual relations with soldiers and sailors a bad thing? (One soldier has written me protesting that servicemen are not responsible for conditions, that the child-girls chase the men and the problem is one of enforcement against them by their parents, not against soldiers and sailors —and there is evidence to support his point.) But is an inhibition against stealing bad? Murder? Indecency? No scientist I have ever encountered in books or person ever contended so. If they did, you and I would know they were wrong.

But the people generally do not always understand these simple obvious common-sense truths. They have not been given that type of leadership by prominent people, yes even by the press, radio and magazines, in the pulpit or in the schools. The loose-running theorists are exerting the preponderant public pressure today — the most popular pressure.

As long as they do, you will have ever increasing juvenile delinquency, and a nation degenerating rapidly in its moral fibre or strength.

PROGRESSIVE PAGANISM

4

PROGRESSIVE PAGANISM

A LEADING child welfare authority diagnoses the juvenile delinquency problem in a labor magazine somcthing like this:

Children feel that they have been pushed around by the war, that they are "in trouble," and this "trouble" is due to a spiritual hunger.

Now I hesitate to take issue, as an amateur, with so eminent and experienced a professional leader, but I would like to submit to her, and to those many readers interested approvingly in my recent columns on the subject — that the main thing wrong with the problem is the attitude she reveals in her diagnosis.

From her own analysis can be gleaned the proof which should convict her of her mistake. She says girls' cases in the courts have swollen 38 percent, boys' 12 percent. Chief girl offensees were, "ungovernable behavior," "running away," and "sex offenses." How in the world does she expect to cure these problems — no matter what else she does — if she coddles the miscreants with the thought that they are just in trouble due to spiritual hunger of their own dear little adolescent selves? Instead of going at it that way, why do we not try to cure "ungovernable behavior," "running away," and "sex offenses" by stronger discipline, including some on parents responsible for such delinquency?

She tells, for example, of a "Julia," whom she describes as "a little 14 year old girl found living with her girlfriend, aged 15, wife of a soldier in a nearby camp. Both girls were having many soldiers visit them each night. The police picked them up one night in a tavern near the camp. Life in her village at home was 'so dull' as compared with life around an army camp."

Dull, huh? Well, that is what Julia told the social workers anyway, but obviously there must be more behind Julia than that in a family background and the lack of discipline or respect for it in either the home, school, or church. Julia got away with this explanation to my friend, the authority, who only asks in her article: "Must the fun children have always be dangerous?"

Apparently so. Sixty-one percent of all the recent burglaries, robberies, and hold-ups in Seattle, she then says, were committed by youths from nine to 16, who, no doubt, find life dull at home.

My complaint is that to look at the problem that way invites juvenile delinquency, creates the excuse for all the little Julias, who, after all, have minds of their own and have learned to get around doting parents and social workers.

Spiritual hunger? Is that what really caused Julia to embark to the camp and the boys to start robbery as a career? They may have thought it, but they are adolescents, and if the free expression of their own little minds is going to be any guide in national handling of the problem, I wouldn't say the nation was being furnished the best possible leadership.

"Julia" does not sound genuine to me. But say there is a "spiritual hunger" on the part of the young, a genuine hunger which causes juvenile delinquency. Even admit Julia had it. Is a lax fondling attitude toward her crime going to make it any better, or is it going to encourage other little Julias to think they can get by with the same story, or at least will not suffer the effects of stern discipline? I do not know what the answer for all spiritual hungers is, but I know where I would start looking — in a church, not around army camps. That is where most adults would start to look for it, and my point is that the time has come to let the adult outlook on the problem prevail over the child outlook.

My friend, the expert's recommendations for cures run along this line: A nation at war must assume responsibility, make up for the absence of fathers and big brothers, and — these are exact quotes — "compensate the children for mothers required to work, for the loss of their time and attention," "keep schools open," "maintain social services," "open new social centers."

I do not believe any of those things will do the job, but I think a change of attitude on the part of this child leader might.

POLICE LEADERSHIP

5

POLICE LEADERSHIP

TWO newspapers publishing my column have complained strongly (threatening to quit) because I have paid too much attention to juvenile delinquency. They thought it a problem to be guided alone by physician writers who advised parents, and I suspect that, behind their complaints, is the common notion that "freedom of expression" will continue to be the song of this era instead of discipline in home, school, and church. In fact, a Pennsylvania reform school superintendent observed that my efforts to swim against a surface tide would await a reward in Heaven, as none was possible on this earth. I disagree.

This juvenile delinquency decadence of our nation is not a child problem or a medical problem. It is a national symptom of a social degeneration involving adults more than children, the first crack that is widening before our eyes in a break of our established culture. If it is not cured in the right way, we will fall down the abyss forecast by the philosophers Spengler and Sorokin, who surmised that western culture was going fast and would result in the rise of a new leadership, possibly oriental (since leadership in world culture has travelled west). Certainly no nation is stronger than the character of its women and children, no matter how many battleships and planes it may have.

No less an experienced expert than Inspector Walter M. Germain, Crime Prevention Police, at Saginaw, Michigan, has recognized juvenile delinquency as a character defect. For some years, he has been speaking and writing of his experience, saying the only alternatives are the building of character or prisons. He even joins a physician writer in prophesying "a psychopathic breakdown of civilization" unless the current march of crime by adolscents is reversed.

His theories of what should be done only partly coincide with mine, yet police are furnishing excellent leadership in some localities like Saginaw. In Morristown, New Jersey, for instance, Detective Lieutenant Valerin went to the mayor with the old familiar story that there was not much police could do about juvenile delinquents until crime was committed except to notify parents of damages due, etc. The mayor suggested a plan of police action leadership. Lieutenant Valerin called in 20 boys and their parents. They founded an organization known as the Junior Legion of Honor. The kids like it. A playground has been set aside for them, and character leadership has been established under older boys. As a result of this alone, the local paper says Morristown now has no juvenile delinquency problems which face other communities. Here, discipline was obtained by wise leadership and example.

How the foolish theorists can continue to advocate the freedom of expression in the face of such obvious evidence of the critical necessity for the establishment of national youth character is more than I can understand. Adults must practice repressions and restraints against animal inclinations and appetites in their own lives, although some do it little better than the juveniles. Until the child mind itself can develop to the point of similar practice, obviously he must have leadership by example and discipline — through a renewal of the waning responsibilities of home, school, and church, to which now may be added, police.

The two editors can quit if they want to. My desk will continue to be a clearing house for such information as long as there is the slightest chance it may be helpful in transmitting information to serve as a guidance for new understanding and action on the problem.

"LET THEM EAT CAKE"

6

"LET THEM EAT CAKE"

ANOTHER thing: Teachers testify in letters to me that parents are only half to blame for the current juvenile revolution. The other half can be traced right to the door of Teachers College, Columbia University, New York, and its responsibility for undisciplined education.

There was spawned and propagated the theory that a child should be given full, uninhibited expression of his impulses and there the whole theory of education was geared to this free expression.

"Educators" who want notoriety, and desire to be classed as "Progressives" and "leaders in the new educational field," took up and popularized the notion that kids should not be required to work. You have heard them: "Children must be made to like school"

. . . "They must be allowed to express themselves and to find hidden talents" . . .

Tests are made out by the teachers nowadays which can hardly do otherwise than develop a nation of graduated half-wits. The questions are not questions, but statements concerning the school work, and all the pupil is required to do is to write "true" or "false." Any child who knows only these two words of the English language, with reasonable luck, must get 50 percent, and if he covered half the class work, a normal guessing ability would give him at least a passing mark of 75 percent. Why study?

Another farce of Progressive education: The teachers write half a sentence and then list three or four possibilities for ending it, inviting the child to select the correct one. The teachers do all the work. The pupil merely puts in a check, so as not to strain — or use — his poor little brain, although the primary reason for education is to teach people to think.

Fanciest, however, was the method of teaching reading "so the child will love to read." Never bother about spelling, pronunciation, or grammar, or anything difficult — that will come. Well, it has not. Instead, there has come a popular intelligent juvenile realization that study and work are not necessary, and teachers have no authority. (Most who write to me are obviously afraid of schoolboards and parents to the extent they dare not challenge a wayward pupil, or let their names be used by me.)

How a leading nation of the modern world could degenerate intellectually to this extent is difficult to imagine. Not even Russia — backward, Communist Russia — has clung to such educational inanities. An educational writer currently reports Russian schools have dropped Progressive education and put the kids to work with stern discipline and thorough scholarship (even eliminating co-education in order that the normal super-interest of romance and marriage be *not* confused with education but left for other hours). If Russia raises her children in this way, and we continue to raise ours in our way, which next generation will be able to stand in this world of conflict? Which nation will survive? What can this war victory bring to us?

We had better quickly give back to the school principals and teachers a disciplinary authority which will command respect. For children raised under proper parental discipline, it is not necessary, and never was. It is the child who does not encounter discipline at home, who must be taught it at school. But the panty-waist Progressive educators say (and unthinking parents also): "You will instill fear in the poor little dears."

Of course. How else? Is not the fear of jail and punishment by society, including ostracism from friends and neighbors, considered necessary to require adult conformity to the laws of society? If necessary for adults who are supposed to have fully developed minds and have learned self-restraint, how much more necessary it is to instill fear of punishment in undeveloped minds.

A Philadelphia psychiatrist who studied 19,000 juvenile court cases there, found just one general cause — "lack of sense of responsibility for behavior." He sees only one cure—discipline. He says only "dilettante psychiatrists" counsel against the instilling of fear of punishment. I would add that the Progressive educational leaders have no ground in modern psychiatry, modern psychology, or ultra-modern common-sense to justify the stupid mistake into which they have drawn the schools and parents of this nation perilously.

WISE YOUTH LEADERSHIP

7

WISE YOUTH LEADERSHIP

PROGRESS is being made toward rejuvenation of juvenile discipline in home, school, and church. The mayor of a large southern city tells me he noticed it at a recent Parent Teachers meeting, called to consider the breaking of windows, slashing of seats, pulling of trolleys in street cars by school children. The note of the meeting was: "We have gone too far in developing self-expression. We must turn to discipline." He had not heard that in such gatherings before.

I can see it also in my mail from all classes, all sections. A great many civic leaders have taken up the trend toward intelligent modern promotion of integrity and character. A Fort Wayne News-Sentinel editor took the whole juvenile delinquency problem to his high school classes in sociology. After full study and discussion, they reached the same conclusion as the PTA. Society, they said, is too willing to condone questionable actions on the part of both adults and children. Our valued freedom of expression, they concluded, has not been accompanied by a parental care in teaching children to live up to the responsibilities that go hand in hand with freedom. Both school and church also are responsible, they added, urging school leadership to develop a set of standards to establish character and integrity—development of child interest in hobbies, religion, choosing of good friends, etc. These Fort Wayne high school sociologists are thus furnishing leadership in their own community which makes column writing of secondary importance when compared with such practical, effective, direct action.

But there is much to be done and undone. Right here in Washington, the Public Welfare Director, Milo F. Christiansen, has submitted proposals which, to my mind, are prime examples of how *not* to do the job. Mr. Christiansen wants $1,000,000 for more mid-city playgrounds, $291,854 for 10 more recreational areas, $1,135,000 for the first year's cost ($75,000 annually thereafter) for swimming pools and night illumination of recreational centers. This is a politician's way. Mr. Christiansen is not a politician, but he is following the political way in this instance.

If money could buy integrity and character for children or adults of this nation, no sum could be too large to spend. But the evidence of all human kind justifies the contrary conclusion. Economies often instill personal integrity and character, but money generally corrups youth. The boys and girls of Fort Wayne, in my opinion, know more about the problems than the District Welfare Director, or at least have proposed a more sensible solution.

If Mr. Christiansen got all his millions for playgrounds, he would still have the problems of disciplinary laxities among parents, in schools and churches. He would not have even touched the root of the trouble. Indeed, juvenile delinquency can flourish as much on playgrounds as in street cars, if children continue to be improperly developed and misled there into free expression of their little animal selves.

Let Mr. Christiansen ask himself before he spends a taxpayer's dollar: Why is it that this nation now, with all its newly made playgrounds, the best in the world, has a juvenile delinquency problem approaching national moral degeneration in its scope, whereas we had no such problems 20, 50, 100 years ago, when children had to make their own playgrounds?

LADY BARFLIES

8

LADY BARFLIES

EVIDENCE is mounting in the daily news columns that parental and child delinquency is traceable to the saloon. No doubt the prohibitionists soon will be taking up that phase and advocating another era of bootlegging, crime, and corruption as a cure.

A Congressional committee has, for instance, heard a policewoman tell of mothers taking babies into saloons for the evening. A great growth of child drunkenness is apparent to the police, and sober children are coming into saloons to bring mama home — a reversal of the old theme of the daughter who came for father and sang: "Father, dear father, come home with me now."

The Portland Oregonian has made an excellent survey showing the part of liquor in delinquency, a part which has caused Domestic Judge Bronn there to advocate a law of holding parents criminally responsible for neglect of children. The problem, no doubt, exists nationally.

Yet to me, this liquor phase is no different than any of the others, and is only an effect, *not* a cause of the trouble. The drinking of alcohol is a custom to which man has subscribed since long before Christianity. The handling of the drunkenness problem through all the ages has been founded on self-restraint, popular scorn, popular disgrace, and such regulatory influences — not prohibition. Obviously, for the average healthy person, a moderate consumption of alcoholic beverages never has been considered harmful by the vast majority of the people of the world — or I believe by most medical men. Overdoses are not only harmful but poisonous, as harmful as any overdoses of medicine which kills.

Foreign nations seldom have our troubles. In their national customs, they generally promote beer and wine, and raise their children to a proper repugnance of drunkenness. In France, Germany and England, for instance, drunkenness has never existed on the scale encountered here. Primarily then, what we need is leadership — and discipline — along similar lines.

Instead, we have gone the opposite way. When prohibition was repealed, most of our political leaders promised there would be no return of the saloon. We not only returned it, but we invited females into it. The facilities provided for man's failing has thereby been extended to women, with the results found in Washington, Portland, and nationally as described above. The institution of separate saloons might be corrective, if any saloons are necessary at all. Hours of operation could be adjusted to discourage drunkenness as in England and Canada. Cheap dives along the roads, known as roadhouses, could easily be regulated out of existence — without prohibition. Also, in most foreign nations, a strong ale is promoted, and it is their working man's drink. Its price is kept cheap; whiskey and strong drinks are made costly. Drinking out in the open in sidewalk cafes, etc., is encouraged in a way differing much from the American booth and dance-hall system.

Certainly present conditions are unsatisfactory and solutions must be sought, but unless those who advocate common-sense correctives take the leadership, we probably will again be plunged into the mistakes of prohibition.

THE BASIC ARGUMENT

9

THE BASIC ARGUMENT

BEST possible claims for Progressive education — which I say has inspired juvenile delinquency and threatened the future of this republic — have been presented by an old friend, Mr. Don Ewing, associate editor of the *Shreveport Times*. He is not a pearl-vest social educator or Gideon Planish. He is not bowed down by any political school board interested in selling newer textbooks for what there is in them — but not necessarily between the covers. He is an intelligent, sincere believer, and his main challenging point to me can be boiled down to this:

"Children must not be forced into a subject until they are ready for it mentally. To read, speak and write English, the child must be fully at ease in parsing grammar. Does a child not better understand the value of a cotton gin by seeing it in operation than by memorizing the date of the inventor? Wouldn't you prefer in every subject — except spelling and mathematics — to teach by demonstrating and observing first hand, instead of memorizing?"

Your theory is that the child merely be exposed to education, that it must not be hard or difficult. It assumes that every child is just dying to absorb education if merely exposed in a kindly way, and if it is made easy for him.

Now you and I know, and everyone else who ever went to school knows this is not true. Human beings are not made that way, child or adult. School is a child's work. There may be a few in every class who will work whether or not it is required, but not the average human being.

Would your Progressive educators train a football team not to tax its energies? Or urge it to use its utmost energies? Do you think our army and navy would be facing victory today if merely exposed to training in a kindly way instead of going through the difficult grind of thoroughly absorbing every detail of every fighting weapon and method better than our enemies have learned them? Which lessons of life have you learned best, the hard ones or the easy ones? What business could succeed under that theory? What anything?

Where did anyone ever get the idea that a child's mind is any different from an adult in its eagerness for work? Psychiatrists and mothers will tell you the average six months old baby can outsmart the average mother (knows when to cry and how to get what he wants by trickery and otherwise).

These Progressive educators, therefore, are not modernists but old-fogeys because they do not know the human mind or human nature. Their premise is wrong. their basic theory is unworkable.

Education is simply teaching people how to think. The specific information you receive in school is generally of little value in after life (probably of less personal value than what you learn outside the classrooms by personal association which contributes more to developing your way of life). The only way to teach our youngsters to think is to require them to improve their minds, not to accept them as they are. Memorizing is something that no one can circumvent by bulling his way through in school. You have to learn it or you do not pass. Your mind may not absorb all the meanings, but it must work to memorize. The more difficult this may be for a youngster, the more improvement that will be wrought in him.

Now do not tell me, Don, that you and your Progressive educators never bulled your way through subjects with a teacher. Personally, I found I could talk myself around practically every subject except Latin. That was the one which I could not get easily. I was required to keep at it by my own fear-shame of quitting. That was the standard then. Under your theory, there would have been no shame, and I would have quit. Now I know that my required application on that subject taught me more about how to think than the subjects I learned more easily.

This is a hard world, Don. The way to prepare a person or a nation to survive in it is not by encouraging laziness. Nothing worthwhile in life has ever been achieved the easy way — education, success, victory in wars. Do you think the Russians are going to educate their coming generation that way? Or the British with their high educational standards which have made that small nation a superior one through generations?

Progressive education will fall just as its related popular doctrine of "the easy way" will fall. No one will kill it. It will die of its own fulfillment just as all other false conceptions must die at the inevitable bastion of nature. If it runs its trend, it will make us the soft, ease-loving, anti-working, anti-exertion people that have always fallen in history before energetic, hardworking, success-striving people. That end is already being prophesied for us by our outstanding philosophers who see no other end possible for our long run.

We have now one belated chance to awaken and modernize our theories and one place we could modernize is in education, not just in the few Progressive education schools, but in all schools where the false theories of your doctrine have inspired a lack of discipline, an easing of requirements, and "The Easy Way."

THE TEACHERS SPEAK

10

THE TEACHERS SPEAK

THE Progressive Educators are trying to turn off the evidence of what they have done to American youth — evidence on the front pages of the newspapers daily in juvenile delinquency developments — as the inaccurate criticism of an ignorant columnist, meaning me. They are writing letters to the papers along that line, issuing interviews to some teachers' publications.

Contrariwise, teachers in a large number of schools have stealthily thumbtacked my columns to their bulletin boards with underscorings and "Amens" mysteriously pencilled in. Teachers and PTA magazines have been reprinting the columns. School boards are writing in for more and back copies. Educators are requesting them by the hundreds for distribution (requests I cannot fulfill). And the mail from college professors, principals, schoolboardsmen, and teachers has piled in daily for the past month with detailed examples of the sorry condition of American education, saying much worse things about it than I have related. All I said was we are raising a nation of half-wits. The evidence indicated I over-estimated the fraction by possibly 50 percent.

Now here is a disclosed struggle between educators of which the public is not generally aware. On top in many towns apparently are the Columbia Teachers College groups preaching their "Take it easy, children" methods, "Don't work too hard," "We will make education interesting for you." On the other hand, are the great bulk of the teachers of the country, sick at heart at the results of this lax system, disillusioned, frightened at the big education trust hanging over them. They write: "Do not use my name." They send me clippings showing what the Big Trust is saying about me, and add such notes as: "This so-called educator is a political hack foisted off on us by the local political machine."

What to do? For the first thing, let everyone know that the campaign of the Progressive educators is false. Criticism of the educational system was not concocted by "a columnist." It existed, and a columnist discovered it for the general public, not for those of the teaching profession who have long participated in the struggle to correct the wrongs, laxities which have put pupils beyond their reach with either learning or discipline. This side-tracking of the issue is a common political trick. The "ins" always attempt to hold their jobs by pretending all is well, that anyone who dares suggest otherwise is unworthy of notice.

In this case, it cannot deceive anyone. The fact that there has been a breakdown in our standards of education and in discipline generally is too obvious to all parents. If the Progressives attempt to maintain themselves by this method, they must eventually lose their skins. A wiser technique for them would be to say: "Let's see what corrections can be made."

In the second place, I shall write one more column containing more evidence of the breakdown in educational standards — evidence obtained only from educators. It will be published tomorrow.

But what else? I think there should be a Congressional investigation of the situation. A complete job being too vast for a columnar undertaking (my primary interest is juvenile delinquency of which education is only one phase), it must be done by authorities empowered to drive the Gideon Planishes out of teaching leadership. The danger of a Congressional investigation is that it, too, would be political. Perhaps a moderate such as Dr. Robert M. Hutchins, President of Chicago University, might bring the necessary impetus to bear to break the trust. Perhaps educational investigating boards in the states and cities, or the PTAs could accomplish something. Possibly a Presidential commission, working as the Wickersham Commission did on prohibition, might furnish the hickory stick.

Whatever is needed to break this political educational racket or laxity must be done, and done by educators themselves. A movement along that line would be popular. It is time to start.

THE PLAIN EVIDENCE

11

THE PLAIN EVIDENCE

IF ANYONE tries to tell you the American schools have not broken down in both scholarship and discipline, cite to them these following facts:

The Navy found incoming freshmen at the leading universities so far below its educational standards, it had to institute the V program. In a test to 4,200 freshmen at 27 leading universities, 68 percent were unable to pass the arithmetic test, and 62 percent failed the whole test. Among the same candidates for Naval Reserve Officers training, only 10 percent had taken elementary trigonometry in highschools, only 23 percent had more than a year and a half of math.

But, in order to enroll the number of men needed by the Navy, Admiral Nimitz wrote in a letter to Prof. Bredvold of the University of Michigan, November 12, 1941, that "it was found necessary at one of the training stations to lower the standards in 50 percent of the admissions."

Not half the graduates of the elementary schools in Tennessee today can read and write well. The condition is exposed in an article in the Tennessee Teacher, by

School Superintendent H. I. Callahan, who says: "The testimony of highschool principals and teachers bears witness to the fact that more than half the children finishing the eighth grade in Tennessee schools are unable to read with ease, comprehension, and pleasure; that they are very poor in the elementary mechanics of written English involving the simpler phases of capitalization, punctuation, and paragraphing . . . ."

It is impossible to teach the products of lax elementary schools a foreign language in college, Dr. T. Braxton Woody, University of Virginia School of Romance Languages, says: "As the sorry products of Progressive Education filter into our classrooms, the problem of what to do with them becomes more and more acute. It is really unreasonable to expect them to learn a foreign language since our modern educators have failed lamentably in their efforts to sugar-coat the pill (of learning)."

If the parent will sit down with his highschool child one night, he will find the average cannot figure the area of a floor if the sides are given in feet and inches; cannot name three countries in every continent; they would not know the capitols of six states, or five rivers in the U.S. or any country. (A Philadelphia teacher, name withheld) . . . Teachers are required to pass pupils even if they do not do the work and this has created a generation of lazy, spineless boys. (Philadelphia teacher) . . . "I know a fine city superintendent who was ousted because he stood for the old-fashioned type of schooling, and another more 'open minded' was selected to make schooling easier." (An Iowa School

Superintendent) . . . The situation is due to "the educational trust, or racket, for this is what the public school administrators, together with Teachers College, add up to," testifies Dr. L. H. Rittenhouse, Haverford College. "The leading educators are interested in enrollments, surveys, teachers credits, new fangled subject and textbooks, publishers, palaces of education" (xxx) "to the neglect of sound disciplinary and moral training"... "Restrictions are necessary... There is no easy road to education," President Jenkins, Georgia Military College... Progressive schools do not produce young men valuable to the army, since their lack of discipline at an earlier time produced a frame of mind that caused them to look with resentment upon military discipline (Junior College of Connecticut).

But best summing up of the situation is by a department head of one of the largest junior colleges in California, who discovered:

"Only one quality in which the student brought up in the new dispensation surpasses his predecessors; he has infinite self-assurance, and shyness is almost nonexistent. But this self-assurance is often a liability for the teacher cannot crack his complacency. Knowing less and less about more and more things, he fails to develop intellectual humility necessary to learning and feels certain he already possesses all the answers. In his ignorance, he is frequently arrogant, and he does not understand the necessity for applying himself to hard tasks that do not strike his passing fancy."

HOW TO THINK

12

HOW TO THINK

Dear Dr. Howard A. Lane, School of Education, Northwestern University:

I WISH you would read again, thoughtfully, your letter to me, and I think you will agree that you have said in effect: "Your writings on Progressive education are incompetent; we are doing exactly what you demand, namely, establishing discipline and scholarship, and teaching the children how to think; only the lunatic fringe of Progressive education does otherwise." You thus denounce me, and accept my purposes at the same time, making them justly applicable only to the lunatic fringe in your midst.

On such a showing, I would accept your conclusions, but I look around me and see evidences of deficient scholarships and disciplinary laxities which seem to require some additional explanation from you. If your educational system is so superior and so perfect, how do these deficiencies happen to occur?

Then, finally, your definition of thinking as "planning action" is astonishing to me. The planning of action is certainly one process of thought, but there are many others. Is the fact that two and two make four a planned action, or is it a memorized truism? And does not the memorizing of that truism by an individual require him to exercise a process of thought which is not planned action but teaches him how to think? Once an individual has learned the processes of thought, he is able to think for himself, and this should be the primary purpose in a Democracy. In a Democracy also, is it not the essential right of all individuals to speak their minds freely, including columnists? How easy it would be to sweep aside all criticism of self by ascribing it to an incompetent source or suppressing it with force as Hitler does. Your proposal to suppress it only with scorn would be dictatorial if you were able to accomplish your objective.

Your system does not require children to use their minds to the utmost of their ability, to acquire the thought processes necessary to allow them to be able to think for themselves. You let their disinclinations fix your standards of teaching. You accept their little minds as they are and adapt your teachings to what they are, rather than attempting to raise them into grander comprehension and greater ability through effort.

I do not think your system should be called "progressive" but might be called "retrogressive," and certainly, undeniably, it is static in theory. It perpetuates a mental status quo.

I suspect you Progressive educators have really only attempted to put education on a wholesale basis, and reduced your standards to the lowest common denominator, just to get in more business, to take in more students, including the mentally incapable. You have gone the way of all business of this age, sacrificing good workmanship and perfection of ideals to mass production. You turn out more students, but not better students—and with this I think in your milder moments, you will agree.

Yours sincerely,

PAUL MALLON

Dear Dr. William Clark Trow, School of Education, University of Michigan:

Personally, I wish I had been granted the privilege of studying under Progressive educators instead of the hard task masters of my day in the public schools and universities I attended. I suspect I would now be a happy somnambulist, able to glean my daily column from the thoughts of others without the effort of attempting to originate from my own mind any provocative, challenging, inspiring thoughts for others. A column of that nature would not, however, sell more than 260 daily newspapers, I suspect. So perhaps I was fortunate in being required to face a rigid, harsh discipline and a standard of scholarship in my schools, which required my little mind to proceed in a direction it would not otherwise have followed if left to its own inclinations. I did not like it then, but I look back on it now with gratitude.

I am afraid you Progressive educators are, therefore, wasting your time trying to convert me, especially with the evidences of your results which I see every day.

Yours sincerely,

PAUL MALLON

THE BREAKDOWN OF CULTURE

13

THE BREAKDOWN OF CULTURE

ONE editorialist has implied that my exposures of the laxities in discipline and scholarship in the schools strike at the heart of Democratic institutions — leaving a reader to suspect that discipline would overthrow Democracy. Now where in the world did he get that idea? The truth is the opposite, as any reasonable man should be able to deduce for himself.

Why did Nazism, Communism, and the Tokio dictatorship rise to their present power in the world? Because they said Democracies were weak, our people undisciplined, and our system deficient? Democracy failed in Germany before Hitler on this very ground. The Weimar republic was a moral forerunner of what weak France later suffered before her fall. The people were not strong, well ordered, but confused and lax in all ways.

I say we shall suffer the same fate unless we mend our easy ways and re-establish discipline in home, school, and church. Juvenile delinquency is only a first crack that shows in our gilt. These are warnings of the degenerating road that is leading on into business (condoning of black markets, etc.) into politics (easy-going acceptance of lack of common integrity and respect for promises) and into personal attitudes of some of our people who have no righteous indignation against cheapness, ignorance, laziness — or even dishonesty. They are more apt to scorn work than crimes against nature. They not only tolerate sloth, they worship it. These are weakneses when we need strength. At the end of this road is dictatorship, not Democracy.

By discipline, I do not mean German heel-clicking, Russian servility, or Tokio bootlicking of an emperor. These critics seem to have forgotten the meaning of Democratic discipline, as well as its operation.

It is only a national standard—a state of national mind—maintained insistently by a majority. It is a custom established by the people themselves. The army and navy do not maintain discipline with a cat-o'-nine tails. They fix a just standard to which all must subscribe, and all save a very small minority of the misguided do subscribe. The guardhouse is maintained for them as a last resort of punishment based on a fair trial under majority Democratic standards and customs.

If you think the example of the army too strained for civilian application, consider how order is maintained in your church. There, you have no guardhouse or sergeant-at-arms, or even written rules of conduct. Yet the sternest discipline is maintained by majority demand. You see very little vandalism, such as carving of seats. Such vandalism would be practically eliminated also in the movie houses, street cars, and other public places where it is now rampant if a majority of this country only firmly insisted. Discipline can be restored to the schools the same way. So can good scholarship. Parents can thus be induced or compelled by scorn alone to take the reins at home, and churches invited to assert themselves again.

This then is the Democratic way of maintaining a strong and orderly nation, and when it fails, you get dictatorship; in fact, you must have dictatorship as a necessary consequence of your own degeneration.

All today who condone the easy-way doctrines, easy learning, easy discipline, who have only sympathy and "understanding" for everything weak, wrong, and inefficient, are the ones who are striking at the heart of Democracy, and will kill it by leading it to its inevitable ruin.

The majority must maintain standards of behavior in home, school, and church, in business, in politics, which will require both children and adults to express their better selves, to study, to work, to develop themselves, to obey, to stop condoning and sympathizing with rottenness and laziness, to eliminate the standard of sloth and ease, to make the nation strong within itself and stronger than its dictator enemies or competitors, or any other nation.

THE OLIGARCHY BREAKS

14

THE OLIGARCHY BREAKS

THE strangle-hold of the "Painless Learning" clique over American schools is breaking fast. The movement for re-establishment of discipline in scholarship and conduct is beginning to succeed on every front. It is being taken up and pushed by foremost educators and teachers who no longer are afraid of their lives, by school boards looking into conditions in their localities, and by Parent Teachers and other civic groups asking for restoration of scholastic common sense.

Pace of the new trend is reflected in the pronouncement of President Robert Sproul of California University. He said in an address (San Francisco, March 23) the Progressive education craze has already run its course, after bringing "the devastation of rampant adolescents," and our "race" to the brink of catastrophe. He blamed the educational publicist, President Eliot of Harvard, for starting the free elective system (students to choose their own subjects) from which "primary and secondary education transferred control of the school in large part from the teachers to the pupils."

For his part, Dr. Sproul announced California has abandoned the elective system in principle and predicted "the disciplined mind, which is the major objective of education, will be sought less and less through undisciplined curriculums." His unchallengeable conclusion: "There is no royal road to learning."

But the incident which makes my heart rise in proudest admiration is the banding together of 26 teachers of the Atlanta Boys High School. They have dared sign their names in an open pronouncement to me, writing, "we have long known the fact stated in your articles, that thousands of teachers are in complete accord with you, but afraid to give their names. We want to take this opportunity to endorse your wise and courageous stand against one of the greatest evils in our country. We are of the opinion that Progressive education is neither progressive nor educational."

There is some of the courage of the signers of the Declaration of Independence in their document to stir the blood and warm the soul. Looking at the Declaration of Independence, you find no facial evidence today of what it might have meant to those who then stood up to be identified. But that kind of courage is as deep in the flesh of America as any of the principles extolled. Others are exhibiting like new courage in their own ways.

"The faculty of the Atlanta Boys High School," they wrote, "has followed your series of articles against Progressive education with great joy and satisfaction. We have long waited for some writer of national importance to take up the cudgel against the dangers of Progressive education.

"This school has tried to hold steadfastly to the fundamental truth that nothing can ever be substituted for the foundation of a building. Likewise, in education, you cannot substitute anything for discipline in the developing of character; and work and achievement cannot be supplanted if a child is to grow into a good citizen. We have watched with a mingled feeling of rage and sadness, as the impotent philosophy of so-called modern education has rotted the moral fibre of our nation."

Then mark well this: "we have listened with wonder and disgust at compulsory assembles, as wordy, bombastic orators spouted out the theory of the 'Freedom of Youth.' We have heard them advocate the development of a youth uninhibited, unworked, and completely disrespectful of all American ideals.

"We must confess we have weakened somewhat from pressure above, and because of the Progressive environment which has been all around us. We have clung to our ideals, however, taking the good and leaving the bad out of the Progressive movement."

America is doing the same. Put these words on your school bullotin boards, teachers, and take heart. The undisciplined educational movement has already broken on the rocks of inquisitive American common sense. I will have more proof tomorrow.

LEARNING IS NOT PLAY

15

LEARNING IS NOT PLAY

IF YOU think the educational trust sponsoring the undisciplined easy way of schooling still easily occupies its mighty seat of fear-dominance, read these following facts: This column is published by 261 daily paying newspapers with a certified circulation of 10,210,585, plus several hundred weeklies of undetermined circulation, and the facts were acquired through these sources.

The National Progressive Education Association (a sort of Chamber of Commerce of Progressive schools) closed and went out of business within the past 30 days. It organized under a new name a few days later. The National Parent Teacher magazine says in the February issue: "Mr. Mallon's keen observations on juvenile delinquency and his approach to the whole problem bring to mind several articles that have appeared recently in this magazine. Whether or not they agree with all Mr. Mallon says, parents and teachers will surely agree that the home is still the cradle of our culture and that discipline should be re-established there on modern psychiatric lines." . . . .The (name omitted) school textbook publishing company has sent a confidential memo to its organization to capitalize on the new trend, saying: "The great difficulty of the past ten years has been that schools have sadly neglected the teaching of fundamentals. Isn't it high time that pupils were properly taught to read, write, spell, figure correctly, and a thorough knowledge of geography and history, which are fundamentals of a sound elementary education?" ....A new member of the San Francisco Board of Education, Garret McEnerney, II, has called for greater emphasis on the three R's, and for public questioning of the educational author of a report on San Francisco teaching methods who pleaded: "All students in the elementary grades should be promoted without examination or test and should ultimately be graduated from the elementary schools whether they possess the requisite knowledge or not, otherwise their characters will suffer"——The Atlanta Journal front-page philosopher "Piney Woods Pete" sums up: "Most children won't study if they ain't made to. And this ain't being done—at school or at home." The Journal performed a superior job of reporting circumstances in some outlying county schools where the pupils teach the teachers by the discussion method (in which the teacher is not allowed to have an opinion). But clear-headed, common-sense Mayor W. B. Hartsfield has little of that in Atlanta where the high school is of the best....The Glen Falls, N. Y. Post-Star says: "Learning is *not* play. It is work. Fine, mature, lasting personal goodness-at-something is not achieved without work, work, work. This truth the education systems must tell the young people. And if the young still will not listen, then education should take them by the collars, slam them down in their seats, and say: "Young ones, we know what is best for you. Now work! . . ." The Raleigh News and Observer counseled the State Education Association convention: "Paul Mallon and his serious charges should not be dismissed by a denunciation. Rather all who are interested in public education, the citadel of Democracy, should ask themselves: Are our schools measuring up to their duty and opportunity; are the children being required to be as thorough as they should in their studies? If not, then the duty of all officials and teachers is first to make a critical examination and take the necessary steps." . . . A hundred school boards, higher educators, principals, preachers, and PTA's have asked and been granted the privilege to reprint my 12 articles so far. You can see them in newspaper files dated December 31, January 14, 17, 25, February 3, 14, 22, 29, March 7, 20, 21, April 4.

The above is just the broth of a ton of evidence which heralds the first turn of the tide. In all, it marks the beginning of the end of the easy way. Such foolishness could not stand in the light of inquiring interest or common sense discussions, both of which are beginning on a national scale. These developments mean teachers need no longer to fear for their lives, indeed that it has become popular to speak out and seek corrections and improvements to re-established discipline in scholarship and conduct in schools, homes, and churches. It will become increasingly popular.

THE COUNTERATTACK

16

THE COUNTERATTACK

DEAR MR.—(Newspaper Publisher): Watch out for your teacher correspondent, Miss G. She is a type beginning to become familiar to me, the kind trying to turn public attention away from the glaring deficiencies in our educational and youth systems by any distraction possible or impossible. I got only as far as her sly question: "Is Mr. Mallon attacking all American schools and institutions?" as quoted in your newspaper, then threw the rest of the clipping away. I do not bother with that kind, which can only represent either intellectual dishonesty or an inability to read plain English. To do so would serve their purposes. They well know what the issue is: the restoration of discipline in both scholarship and conduct in the schools. Let them talk and write about that.

What has happened in education has become quite clear to me. We went into mass production about 12 to 15 years ago. Education got to be big business, and the classroom an assembly line. We sacrificed the ideals of workmanship and scholarship to the ideal of numbers. We got to turning out three or four times as many students, but they were less than half educated.

How could it be otherwise? The standards naturally had to be lowered to take in everyone. We even got so low in a few Progressive Educational schools that today there is no standard either of scholarship or discipline except that established by the children themselves. Grown-up educators, with apparently adult minds, today openly advocate that every child be passed regardless of his mental capacity so he will not personally be "ashamed" of his deficiency. Imbeciles thus fix our standards. Nearly everywhere we have cut our great educational ideals to some extent to cater to the lowest and the worst of our populace.

This sort of thing cannot continue. The people will not stand for it when they see their children not being properly educated, not being taught to think in accordance with their real ability.

Some needed corrections are obvious. The restoration of standards is clearly demanded. In colleges, this can easily be done by abolishing the elective system, allowing educators to fix the courses rather than the student. This has been started already in California University, and must be followed in the high schools where those of sufficient intelligence to hope to go on to college must be required to study fundamentals sufficiently to pass college examinations. It must also be done in grade schools in order to prepare students properly for high school. For those capable of learning, our course then is clear. Scholarship can be restored in this way alone. This way will furnish the beginning of restoration of discipline. Then we will at least develop sufficient leaders to handle our future nation wisely in business, politics, economics; for, from this class of those capable of learning must come our leadership.

As for the rest, I am not so certain. I prefer to believe that the average child in the United States is in the first class, but some educators tell me different. If we are developing such a nation of morons so as not to be able to teach our average child the fundamentals of reading, writing, and arithmetic — if the minds we are spawning are not capable of retaining common education, as some educators say—the future of Democracy and intelligent decisions by the voting masses of the people is certainly a hazardous prospect. I do not believe these claims can be justified except with strained statistics, counting heavily a large class of backwoods illiterates and imbeciles everywhere.

But, in any case, they must be handled in a special way. We must offer the utmost possible schooling to our least educatable class. It must therefore be done in separate classes or separate schools. What their little minds think about such classification is not half as important to this nation as the maintenance of scholarship for those able to learn. This country cannot be sacrificed to its mental deficients.

Another step absolutely essential is the restoration of the right of punishment to the teachers or principals of all schools. Our youth must be required to study and to accept a social line of discipline and conduct established by the majority. Vandalism, hoodlumism, and sloth must be put down by whatever punishment is required. The standard for punishment should be that it must be effective. Parent Teachers Associations must insist upon this. School boards must choose high types of men as principals, men capable of disciplinary leadership in accordance with modern psychiatric understandings.

Above all: Chase the crack-pots out.

Yours sincerely,

PAUL MALLON

THE SOUNDING BOARD TALKS

17

THE SOUNDING BOARD TALKS*

THE Birmingham Teachers Association poll* showed, in a provable, specific instance, the condition of affairs inside the schools of the country — a condition confirmed by my mail from teachers in many cities. It helpfully points a direct way for improvement.

The teachers realize the progressive education theory will not work either with a big "P" or a little "p". The high school teachers, seeing the pupils the grammar schools are sending up to them, ungrounded in fundamental figures-and-facts education, are almost unani-

* The Birmingham Teachers Association Bulletin has just completed a poll of teachers there on the question: "Do you in general agree or disagree with the Paul Mallon articles on education that have recently been appearing in the daily press?" Every tenth teacher whose name appeared in the telephone book was called and assured her name would not be divulged. The Bulletin says: "Four of the teachers hesitated to give their decision, until reminded no names would be used, then said: 'Oh well, I agree with Mr. Mallon then.' "

The poll showed 79 percent of the high school teachers in agreement with me, 22 out of the 28 polled. Only three disagreed and three would not commit themselves.

Of the 50 elementary grade teachers called, 22 were favorable to my position, 16 unfavorable, and nine on the fence. The BTA Bulletin comments: "In general, those who taught the lower grades were nearly unanimous in condemnation of the Mallon articles; while those who taught the higher elementary grades were more likely to agree with him."

As a whole, 56 percent of the teachers agreed, 24 percent disagreed, while 19 percent said they were not familiar with my articles or that they were on the fence and could not say either way.

The BTA Bulletin published its poll under a heading: "Classroom teachers uphold Mallon Criticism" and concluded: "The ones whose actual job it is to do the work do *not* think Progressive Education works."

mously against the progressive education theory in any of the varying degrees which the educational trust has imposed upon them.

So also are the top half of the elementary grades teachers. They see what the first, second, and third grades are sending up to them in the way of uneducatable children.

Among the teachers, only those in the first few grades like the idea of turning school into a kindergarten. There, then, is where the primary fault lies. There is where correction must start.

The fundamentals of education, leading up to both scholarship and discipline must be restored to the lowest grades; otherwise, we will continue to turn out children who have developed only a fraction of their wits. Unless they are started right, the rest of their schooling is a waste of time.

But another part of the poll suggests how difficult that simple solution may be to accomplish. Among the principals polled—the administrators in charge of each Birmingham School—only one principal "agreed with Mr. Mallon" (as the BTA Bulletin puts it), 10 disagreed, and three were on middle ground."

"There is certainly something significant in the almost unanimous opposition of the principals to Mr. Mallon's contentions, while such a high percentage of the classroom teachers agrees with the columnist," the BTA says, then tells what it thinks this significance is:

"Progressive education has gone over big with the administrators, many believe, because it is showy; it can be pictured and advertised in the papers and magazines. A pupil who has made an elaborate scrap book will get more attention than one who has mastered the binominal theorem or learned the underlying causes of the Civil War. The scrap book goes over big at the PTA-Fathers' night, state fairs, and educational conventions."

This is true, but I wonder if there is an additional explanation. The progressive educational group has attempted to break up my business of columning because I got into this question as a sideline public service. They have induced a few editors to quit; others to leave my column out when it speaks on this subject.

They have spread intellectually dishonest misrepresentations about my stand around the country (where they thought I would not detect them, though teachers and parents hasten to give me the evidence by first mail) which would make a Philadelphia ward heeler blush.

Judging from this, I would say they have their invisible yoke on the principals and the school administrators also and maintain it in the same way to keep themselves in their jobs, to sell their own special textbooks, to line up with the local city councils and school boards where they can.

In short, I think they have a corrupt political machine —but even so they cannot down the teachers who know their basic principle is wrong.

I say the teachers will not stand for it much longer, and the parents will not. Villifying me will do them no good. Not until they abandon their wrong principle will they be safe. As the Birmingham Teachers Bulletin says:

"The polls show a great majority of teachers feel very keenly about this question, and many of them gave assurance that they had felt that way for many years. Mr. Mallon, with his advantageous sounding board, has simply put the matter up for unavoidable discussion.

"When history has written a true account of the argument, we feel sure that the fountain head of progressive education will be shown to come from the truism (often ascribed to Dr. Dewey), 'We learn by doing.'

"Of course we do; but the pedagogical enthusiast seized upon the phrase and concluded that everything must be a doing; hence activity school; hence the greater-freedom-for-pupils idea; and hence the resulting breakdown in discipline.

"Progressive education with a capital "P" is definitely going out with the war demand for facts-and-figures education. The champions of "P" are trying to save face by substituting a little "p".

"Fortunately, it can be said there has been very little of the capital "P" in Birmingham; neither has there been any great amount of it over the United States except in spots. The spirit of it has had its effects though. Teachers have been confused, and no teacher can do a good job when she is confused.

"Yes, the pendulum is swinging. We should try to get our bearings when it passes the middle."

Principals and school administrators would do well to read this handwriting on the wall.

RABBIT ROMANTICISM

18

RABBIT ROMANTICISM

AN APPARENT unmarried lady principal of a junior high school rises right up in the April magazine of her Teachers Association and demands point blank:

"Where do we stand?" on sex.

She makes clear where she stands, as follows:

"We in school can no longer ignore our responsibility for cushioning the shock (of sex) with information; for curing the pre-occupation by satisfying curiosity with knowledge; for lightening the load of fear, worry, guilt and shame that so many children carry; for presenting the beauty of life from which comes the literature, poetry, art and music of romantic love . . ."

"Nor can we fail to supply mother substitutes in whom children can confide. Adolescents face certain development tasks with which they need help. Then if ever, they must wage the battle of gradual emanipation from parents" (at junior high school age).

Now here is a well-meaning lady who unwittingly demonstrates her own incapacity to teach the most difficult subject of all human behavior. Her thoroughly nice idea, I assume, is to raise the conceptions of sex to a higher plane.

In short, she would teach "romantic love" under the title of social hygiene. Would this cure juvenile delinquency or mitigate it or make the children any different?

Inasmuch as this subject now seems to have entered school curricula rather generally, it can hardly be termed taboo for common sense discussion. All the children whom Miss Whosis wants to teach her own higher appreciation of romance, collecting their sex secrets as a mother substitute and aiding their emancipation from their parents—all of them have parents who also have their own ideas of romance, sex, mothers and emancipation.

Sex is the most personal problem of human existence. No two people will have precisely the same ideas about it. Attitudes vary as much as individual personalities. Mothers who have any interest in their children at all will insist on raising their children with their own personal notions on these subjects at least.

I doubt if they will stand for Miss Whosis and anyone in school teaching ideas at variance with their own. I know I would not let her teach my child after reading her article which leads me to believe she is not competent on this subject.

Who is competent? Some people say a psychiatrist or a physician. Yet, it is evident their attitudes also differ widely, range the whole course from radicalism to conservatism, from Freudianism to Puritanism. To have them teach sex in the schools would be as unsatisfactory as having the preachers of all religions try to teach their individual religions in the schools.

This movement is part of the whole false philosophy that has seeped into the very blood of this nation in recent years to bring us such problems as juvenile delinquency, declines in discipline and scholarship—the philosophy of free expression, self-indulgence as being good for the individual.

The realities of life are not in accord with that philosophy. The laws of nature and of the land work on a contrary principle, the Christian principle of restraint and discipline. Some of the movie stars who recently have been in the courts can testify to that.

Only fools follow in their actual lives the "pleasure-pain" philosophy of modernism which holds that which causes me pleasure is good and pain is bad. Momentary pleasures can cause a lifetime of pain; whereas out of pain many men have grown strong and great. (Mr. Roosevelt for one.)

What should be taught is discipline, self-discipline, and the placc to teach that first is in the home. That is the reality principle, what is really good for the individual, the community and the nation. That is where we should stand.

Yet such nonsense as Miss Whosis proposes to teach has a hold on the thinking of a large class in this country, and may have to run its course and expose its own futility and stupidity to its advocates before we get back to common sense.

THE DECLINE OF REASON

19

THE DECLINE OF REASON

I HAVE not written lately about progressive education and its share in the responsibility for juvenile delinquency, because everyone else seems to be doing and saying the right things about it.

Every man in the street today knows what is wrong with education. That question was asked of ten persons along the street in Toledo by the Blade's inquiring reporter. The answers were practically all the same:

"I don't believe the young people are getting a good start in arithmetic and spelling. Too much stress on extracurricular activities."

"I believe my son is getting a better general education than I, but more emphasis should be placed on the three R's and on discipline."

"Graduates do not seem to know about simple necessary things like mathematics and spelling."

These words from a railroad man, barber and housewife are practically the same as have been arising from my typewriter since last January.

What we need for a well educated, intelligent, democratic nation (and a cure for juvenile delinquency) is discipline in home, school and church, discipline by all methods, particularly the development of mental discipline and reasoning powers by education which stimulates the thought processes.

A professor friend of mine has a notion, novel to me, as to how we got into this modern mess. It shows the broader scope of the trouble beyond education and juvenile delinquency. His theory is that this century has witnessed a decline in respect for reason.

Our leading philosophers gradually pushed down the theory of common sense reasoning as a way of living and promoted the theory of living by intuition—"Living has value only as it satisfies men's appetites", and such stuff.

Thus have developed such monstrous ogres of unreasoning civilization as Fascism and Communism.

Instead of each man reasoning things out for himself, weighing the factors as he sees them on both sides, and imposing this mass will on our customs and government, we have come into what Hitler in his extremities, calls guidance by emotional fanaticism — he proudly proclaims "fanaticism" over reason. Everywhere we worship instinct instead of thought.

This has been an easy-selling doctrine to the average man. Human nature has made him a creature desiring comfort, ease, luxury. Reasoning things out is hard work. Study requires mental discipline. The average man will not do it, unless education requires it, and unless the whole way of life of the country demands it.

Where you get by intuition and fanaticism is well shown by where Hitler has taken himself and his entire nation.

Our people still have the right to reason for themselves. But in our country, we have been leading up to the intuitional way of life by allowing some fools among our modern philosophers to tell us that we should individually live by the method — following instinct on sex, for instance, instead of reason.

In politics also, we have encouraged emotional leadership, the incitement of hatreds, but, most dangerous of all, we have promoted the herding instinct in government by worshiping totalitarian ways with government control of every phase of life of the individual.

Intuition? That is what guides a dog or a horse. Man was made with a brain, capable of reasoning, capable of developing intelligence. He does not have it when he is born. He will never develop it except by disciplined training which will force him to use his mind.

Education by the method of movie shows and sightseeing will not add to an individual's ability to think a fraction as much as working out one single difficult problem in arithmetic.

"Learn by doing" was what the philosopher James taught. It should be "Learn by thinking and doing."

This is the real bottom basis of what has been wrong, I believe, not only with education but all our moves, our common popular viewpoint.

By following intuitional methods and habits, we could become a nation of morons at the mercy of leaders who alone are allowed to think or who are morons themselves, guided as Hitler by his instincts and fanaticism.

I think that trend has been broken. In the past few months, nearly every newspaper has carried daily accounts of juvenile delinquency meetings guided away from the intuitional theories and toward common sense.

School boards, Parent Teachers Associations, commentators (though not yet the politicians, for some reason I have not yet discerned) are talking and working toward the same goal. Even the recent primaries suggested that people are thinking in politics.

If this new trend persists, the questions of our war debts, international cooperation and internal troubles will lose their horror. There is no problem a reasoning, intelligent nation cannot solve. Intuition can solve nothing.

SEX GOES OUT

20

SEX GOES OUT

THE restoration of common-sense teaching in the schools is proceeding so swiftly (and so silently), the general public is not aware of it.

With the least possible advertising and a minimum acknowledgement of error nationally, the teaching trends of more than a decade are being widely revised.

The false philosophies of progressive education which corrupted the youths and encouraged juvenile delinquency with laxity of discipline, are being corrected, in the east, at least, where all these trends and swings originate.

Do you remember, for instance, the column published May 10? It set forth the ideas of a junior high school principal in Philadelphia, who wanted to teach romantic love to 15-year-old children in special classes on sex hygiene (the lady herself being a "Miss").

I do not know how she made out with her plan, disclosed in an article in the Philadephia Teachers Associations News Letter of April, which said the teachers must lead the gradual emancipation of children from their parents and become "mother substitutes".

But Washington school authorities have just announced they are dropping their class in sexual education entirely. Although it never went as far as to teach "romantic love" and ran only three weeks of the year, it was unanimously conceded a complete failure.

"The boys and girls either laughed or were scared to death," says a wise surgeon and physician member of the Board of Education, Dr. James A. Gannon.

Apparently Boston, Philadelphia, Baltimore and Richmond are taking the same action. Only New York of the five seaboard cities checked by Dr. Gannon will stick to sex education this Fall. They had the same experience as Washington. Dr. Gannon says:

"Teachers as a rule are not temperamentally fitted or competent to give sex instructions. Our experimental session became a circus for the students and an impossible situation for the teachers. You might think physician teachers would be satisfactory, but they are not, because they talk over the heads of children.

"We will dispense with the sex classes which were a part of the physical instruction course and hereafter teachers will merely answer questions as these arise, and furnish in the regular courses, such as biology, such moderate information as is constructive, non-controversial and helpful."

Thus are the views expressed in this column May 10 becoming prevailing and more popular (the idea that human thought is far from perfection on the sex subject, that no one is competent to teach sex which is such a highly personal and individual problem not even psychiatrists have yet accepted an agreed course and no two members of any Board of Education have precisely the same attitude toward sex).

But these views were not popular then. In Boston they were especially criticized. A professor of human relations in the Massachusetts Institute of Technology wrote me that frank sex instruction had reduced stealing in Wisconsin and said:

"Sex is being taught in the schools with great success."

He was so obviously wrong as to make a reply unwarranted. If you could cure stealing with sex instruction, the education should not be limited to 15 year olds.

The truth is, a case history of the sex lives of these progressive educators would probably show them not only incompetent to teach others but even to handle their own adulthood without divorce or other extreme difficulties, which would make them about average for these times.

One physician tells me 90 per cent of his adult cases are founded in similar facts of life. They had better first reach perfection themselves — or at least agree on a common doctrine — before undertaking to impose their ideas on others.

It seems Boston is thinking, taking hold, and acting, and not in the way of radicals. On August 8 the Business Manager for the Boston School Committee said discipline in the schools there was "terrible", demanding correction to cure laxities. August 10 headlines in Boston papers told of a teacher who hired a large boy in her class at 10 cents a day to maintain order because she could not. August 11: "Teachers are afraid to tell the truth against the evil system, fear to lose their jobs, blame superintendents."

All this developed from investigation of the causes of juvenile delinquency, originally traced by this column to laxity of discipline in school, home and church.

The progressive revolution in education, treating children as "poor dears" to be coddled against using their brains, for freedom of expression, against restraint and subjecting them only to pleasant sightseeing education, weekly draws nearer its close.

NEW FOGEYISM

21

NEW FOGEYISM

THE Pepper Sub-committee came up in the Senate some time back with the results of nine months or more of profound study of juvenile delinquency.

The tome had a tone of august severity and it indicated the committee had heard 50 witneses; however it did not say who these witneses were and I would judge from the conclusions that they might have been the children.

The main philosophical conclusion, for instance, was that "children are people." Frankly I always thought they were rather immature people, who needed to be handled, led, inspired—and maybe spanked now and then for their own good, although I know the children mostly object to that.

The report puts the mothers on a high plane also as "good people," and takes the happy slant that the children who are running wild just represent a sign of the times. In fact, as far as I can make out, there is no criticism in the report for anyone, including the delinquents.

As for handling children, the report says such things as "instituting a curfew law, excluding them from motion pictures, sterner discipline or lowering of the juvenile age is unlikely to lead to the heart of the problem."

No, no, you cannot have sterner discipline or deprivations. What must you have, Senator Pepper? I think he must have been grinning in the direction of the election booths when he wrote the answer, after months of study from 50 witnesses.

"The child should be within reach of churches, community centers and youth organizations, where, with other children, he can share his hours of worship, play, recreational activities," he wrote, or rather the report says, if he wrote it, because it sounds a lot like the ladies in the Childrens Bureau of the Labor Department.

I always thought the children could pretty well reach the churches now. There are a lot of them around. Pepper might have made more of a point, the way I look at it, if he had suggested the churches reach the children.

As for reaching the playgrounds, I can see rather clearly what Senator Pepper is reaching for. He wants new ones built, a reach which has often been stretched from Washington carrying funds from the Treasury or from the municipal treasuries.

This may be one answer for child recreation — if more playgrounds are really needed in some localities —but it is also the answer to a politician's dream, more spending.

In precisely the same ethereal political realm, the report unrealistically goes on to point out there are now only 12 Federal agencies handling child problems —so it wants another one.

"The Committee knows of no Federal agency whose services could be dispensed with safely," it concludes. "Neither does the committee know of any Federal agency set up in such a way that it can provide adequate leadership and coordination in the whole broad field of delinquency protection."

This reasoning seems to be a little complex to me. It holds, in short, that while all these bureaus have failed to do anything successfully to cure juvenile delinquency, a cure can be made by another bureau at the top.

It seems to me I have heard that solution before in connection with many other deficiencies and failures of government leadership.

The report recommends that this new commission "for children and young people be established in the Office of War Mobilization" (now that the war is nearly over) and that the new bureau establish "child guidance clinics" as an integral part of the school systems over the country.

For this, it recommends Federal funds for "grants-in-aid to states"—the old money answer again.

There are many other similar conclusions in the report, but I think the most important one behind it was not directly mentioned—namely that an election was scheduled for November 7.

BIGGEST BUSINESS

22

BIGGEST BUSINESS

BIGGEST industry, by far, in the United States is education.

In plant, this nation has invested $14,223,489,985 (1940 figure from the United States Office of Education) compared with a paltry $2,750,000,000 in plant of the No. 1 commercial industry, motor vehicles, bodies and parts.

We have put five times more money into the value of education production buildings from kindergarten through college, than in our vast and fabulous motors production, yet front-page readers rarely notice this leading industry, and people generally pay little attention to it, although they own the stock in it.

Annual operating cost of education is $3,203,547,586 (same source, covering 1941-42) which is more than half the total of wages paid in every other industrial area in 1939. Practically every day you notice strikes and arguments about industrial wages. For those we have labor boards, little steel formulas and great political agitation and interest. In the nation's largest industry, into which the public actually annually pays $2,671,653,202, there is no comparable interest—and no comparable results.

There are other significant distinctions. The nation's largest industry is not run by business men.

County and city officials operate the bulk of it (their taxpayers furnishing $1,826,937,572 for the public schools) while the states furnished $979,539,773; the Federal government $83,338,030 and privately controlled schools spent $551,998,864 (all 41-42 figures).

The Federal government, furthermore, acts vigorously to control inflation and deflation in all industries, excepting only this one, the biggest. A great watch is kept on the security, salaries and management of all businesses, except this one.

The school text book concessions must constitute a tremendous business, but no commissions nationally watch it.

Post-war planning for industry is a primary occupation now, but this one is neglected excepting that more Federal funds for building more schools are to be provided. The industry is practically unrepresented in Washington except for a few lobbying organizations seeking appropriations, and these are not managed by business men—indeed they could not furnish me with the figures above quoted.

I think it is clearly suggested by the outer evidence that this industry is the least well managed, as well as the least attended to.

It is time the stockholders in this business started paying more attention to their investment. It is time also that national leaders, citizens and even government started recognizing the vastness of the industry, its financial influence, its economic effects, as well as the efficiency of its production, rather than leaving all this authority and control spread around loosely and not only uncontrolled but unadvised in various uncoordinated hands.

It is time also that the workers in that industry, the teachers, realize that they are in the largest industry and more aggressively protect their economic rights and defend their leading political and economic position.

I certainly do not mean by this that they should join a union, and particularly not a union nationally or internationally controlled by workers in lesser industries or their leaders, and pay tribute with high initiation fees and dues for the privilege of such leadership, which might be far from the best with which they could provide themselves.

For any group involving intellectual differentiations and attainments, I do not believe unions answer the need for leadership. For girls in a factory doing uniform work at the same machines, the leveling process of unionism fits well. But for teachers, doctors, lawyers, writers—professions in which the ideal of individual achievement must be maintained and brilliance rewarded—I do not favor unionization, but I do favor the earnest search for wise leadership.

So I think the teachers should seek the wisest possible direction, politically and economically, a democratic leadership based on superiority of ability, rather than placing their cause upon the ground of sheer numbers as unions so often do. They are not masses, but individual personalities, capable of finding a joint expression in a way they will enjoy more and which should better serve their particular interests.

Index

Index—Continued

Index—Continued